Dependable Moneymakers

investments in profitable
mutual funds for retirement
prosperity

King Anthony Kovacs

DEPENDABLE MONEYMAKERS

Since the mutual fund inceptions, all 29 mutual funds attained outstanding investment performance. These mutual funds are dependable moneymakers because most years were gains to investors and few years of losses!

DEPENDABLE MONEYMAKERS

Knowing and understanding the fundamentals in this book helps achieve goals of prosperity for retirement and or savings portfolios. The proof that each mutual fund is a dependable moneymaker is based on the annual performance returns and can be easily verified using the reference source. Every mutual fund's performance exceeds the investment category averages.

The financial information provided is accurate, dependable, and thorough. The author does not assume and, at this moment, refuses liability for possible human error.

There are no guarantees of future results. The material and data presented in this paperback are for informational purposes only. Book purchase go to: www.amazon.com/dp/B0CSKFXL9V

DEPENDABLE MONEYMAKERS

CONTENTS:

DEPENDABLE MONEYMAKERS

Twenty-Nine Profitable Mutual Funds

List of essential information is included in each mutual fund report to assist you in making an investment:

Investment Category Description

Investment Policy

Mutual Fund Name & Ticker Symbol

Contact (800 number, address, website)

Mutual Fund Details

Top 10 Holdings

Mutual Fund 5-Year Returns

Mutual Fund Investment Category

1, 3, 5, 10-years Performances

Category Rank

Average Performance Comparison

ALTERNATIVE GLOBAL MACRO

Investment Policy: The fund seeks high total return over the long term by allocating its assets among stocks, bonds, and short-term instruments. Within each of these classes, the fund may invest in both domestic and foreign securities.

Delaware Ivy Asset Strategy Fund A-WASAX

888-923-3355
www.delawarefunds.com

12/29/23   NAV: $20.17 Return: 15.61%%

Delaware funds
2005 Market Street
Philadelphia, PA 19103

FUND DETAILS:

Open to all investors

Risk: high

Minimum Investment Purchase: $750

Maximum Front End Sales: 5.75%

Net Expense Ratio: 1.15%

Inception Date: July 10, 2000

Number of Years of Gains: 15

Number of Years of Losses: 8

TOTAL NET ASSETS: $1.7 Billion

TOP 10 HOLDINGS:

Microsoft Corporation
Amazon.com Incorporated
Apple Incorporated
Alphabet Incorporated
Vanguard Russell 2000 Index ETF Shares
MasterCard Incorporated
Xtrackers USD Hi Yield Corp Bond ETF
Taiwan Semiconductor Manufacturing Co Limited
Intuit Incorporated
Salesforce, Incorporated

FIVE-YEAR RETURNS:

Year: 2023
Net Asset Value: $20.17 12.37%
Dividend Distribution: 0.58% 3.24%
Total Return: 15.61%

Year: 2022
Net Asset Value: $17.95 -26.5%
Dividend Distribution: $3.20 13.1%
Total Return: -13.40%

Year: 2021
Net Asset Value: $24.43 2.0%
Dividend Distribution: $2.81 11.7%
Total Return: 13.70%

Year: 2020
Net Asset Value: $23.95 9.3%
Dividend Distribution: $0.64 2.9%
Total Return: 12.2%

Year: 2019
Net Asset Value: $21.92 6.7%
Dividend Distribution: $1.25 6.1%
Total Return: 12

MUTUAL FUND RETURNS:

1-year Return: 15.61%

Average Investment: 8.54%%

Investment Rank: 10

3-year Return: 5.30%

Average Investment: 2.30%

Investment Rank: 19

5-year Return: 8.18%

Average Investment: 4.85%

Investment Rank: 5

10-year Return: 3.79%

Average Investment: 2.88%

Investment Rank: 31

3, 5, and 10-year Return annualized

ALTERNATIVE LONG/SHORT EQUITY

Investment Policy: The fund seeks long-term capital appreciation. It invests primarily in both long and short positions in equity securities principally traded in U.S. markets. This sub-advisor seeks to be fully invested in the long portfolio, while allowing the size of the short portfolio to fluctuate based on the market opportunity.

Invenomic Fund; Investor-BIVRX
855-466-3406
www.invenomic.com

12/29/23 NAV: $19.32   Return: 16.22%

Invenomic Capital Management
211 Congress St. - floor 8
Boston, MA. 02110

FUND DETAILS:

Open to all investors

Risk: high

Minimum Investment Purchase: $5,000

Maximum Front End Sales: no load

Net Expense Ratio: 3.18%

Inception Date: June 19, 2017

Number of Years of Gains: 6

Number of Years of Losses: 0

TOTAL NET ASSETS: $138.40 million

TOP 10 HOLDINGS

Comcast Corporation
Verizon Communications, Inc
AT&T, Inc.
Zoom Video Communications, Inc.
Penn Entertainment, Inc.
Expedia Group, Inc.
Viatris, Inc.
SS&C Technologies Holdings, Inc.
Lyft, Inc.
eBay, Inc.

FIVE-YEAR RETURNS:

Year: 2023
Net Asset Value: $19.32 -3.45%
Dividend Distribution: $3.94 19.67%
Total Return: 16.22%

Year: 2022
Net Asset Value: $20.01 16.00%
Dividend Distribution: $5.69 32.99%
Total Return: 48.99%

Year: 2021
Net Asset Value: $17.25 40.24%
Dividend Distribution: $2.50 20.33%
Total Return: 60.57%

Year: 2020
Net Asset Value: $12.30 7.80%
Dividend Distribution: $0.38 3.33%
Total Return: 11.13%

Year: 2019
Net Asset Value: $11.41 7.84%
Dividend Distribution: $0.37 3.50%
Total Return: 11.34%

MUTUAL FUND RETURNS:

1-year Return: 16.22%
Average Investment: 10.70%
Investment Rank: 25

3-year Return: 41.93%
Average Investment: 6.01%
Investment Rank: 2

5-year Return: 29.65%
Average Investment: 7.05%
Investment Rank: 2

10-year Return: --
Average Investment: --
Investment Rank: --

3, 5, and 10-year Return annualized

ALTERNATIVE MANAGED FUTURES

Investment Policy: The fund seeks to achieve long turn capital appreciation. The fund makes a combination of investments directly in in actively managed fixed income portfolio, and indirectly through its wholly owned subsidiary in trading companies that employ the managed futures program of Campbell and Company, Inc.

Campbell Systematic Macro A – EBSAX
888-838-0770
www.rbbfund.com

12/29/23   NAV: $8.89 Return: -2.12%%

Rbb Fund Inc.

615 E. Michigan St.

Milwaukee, WI 53202

FUND DETAILS:

Open to all investors

Risk: High

Minimum Investment Purchase: $2,500

Maximum Front End Sales: 3.50%

Net Expense Ratio: 2.00%

Inception Date: March 1, 2013

Number of Years of Gains: 6

Number of Years of Losses: 3

TOTAL NET ASSETS: $941.7 million

TOP 10 HOLDINGS:

There are no companies listed on the Internet. This information is only available in the mutual fund's prospectus

FIVE-YEAR ANNUAL RETURNS:

Year: 2023
Net Asset Value: $8.89 -3.47%
Dividend Distribution: $0.12 1.35%
Total Return: -2.12%

Year: 2022
Net Asset Value: $9.21 13.84%
Dividend Distribution: $1.39 17.18%
Total Return: 31.02%

Year: 2021
Net Asset Value: $8.09 1.76%
Dividend Distribution: $0.57 7.17%
Total Return: 8.93%

Year: 2020
Net Asset Value: $7.95 3.11%
Dividend Distribution: $0.00
Total Return: 3.11%

Year: 2019
Net Asset Value: $7.71 -5.98%
Dividend Distribution: $1.43 17.44%
Total Return: 11.46%

MUTUAL FUND RETURNS:

1-year Return: -2.12%
Average Investment: -1.55%
Investment Rank: 44

3-year Return: 12.61%
Average Investment: 7.25%
Investment Rank: 11

5-year Return: 10.48%
Average Investment: 5.89%
Investment Rank: 6

10-year Return: 4.36%
Average Investment: 2.96%
Investment Rank: 24

3, 5, and 10-year Return annualized

CONVERTIBLE SECURITIES

Investment Policy: The fund seeks to provide long-term capital appreciation, emphasizing protecting capital during unfavorable market conditions. Based on historical evidence, the Manager believes that market return/risk characteristics differ significantly across market conditions.

Fidelity Convertible Securities Fund - FCVSX
877-208-0098
www. Fidelityfunds.com

12/29/23   NAV: $32.44   Return: 11.42%

Fidelity Convertible Securities
82 Devonshire St.
Boston, MA 02109

FUND DETAILS:

Open to all investors

Risk: above average

Minimum Investment Purchase: N/A

Maximum Front End Sales: no load

Net Expense Ratio: 0.72%

Inception Date: January 5, 1987

Number of Years of Gains: 28

Number of Years of Losses: 8

TOTAL NET ASSETS: $1.6 billion

TOP 10 HOLDINGS

Wells Fargo & Company
Bank of America Corp.
NextEra Energy Inc.
Apollo Global Management Inc.
DHT Holdings Inc.
AES Corp
Chart Industries, Inc.
Frontline PLC
Walt Disney Co.
NVIDIA Corp.

FIVE-YEAR RETURNS:

Year: 2023
Net Asset Value: $32.44 9.74%
Dividend Distribution: $0.50 1.68%
Total Return: 11.42%

Year: 2022
Net Asset Value: $29.56 -19.28%
Dividend Distribution: $1.13 3.09%
Total Return: -16.19%

Year: 2021
Net Asset Value: $36.62 -7.90%
Dividend Distribution: $7.42 18.66%
Total Return: 10.76%

Year: 2020
Net Asset Value: $39.76 26.02%
Dividend Distribution: $4.30 13.63%
Total Return: 39.64%

Year: 2019
Net Asset Value: $31.55 25.75%
Dividend Distribution: $1.02 4.07%
Total Return: 29.82%

MUTUAL FUND RETURNS:

1-year Return: 11.42%
Average Investment: 8.90%
Investment Rank: 16

3-year Return: 2.00%
Average Investment: -1.94%
Investment Rank: 11

5-year Return: 15.09%
Average Investment: 10.50%
Investment Rank: 3

10-year Return: 8.05%
Average Investment: 7.33%
Investment Rank: 32

3, 5, and 10-year Return annualized

EQUITY INCOME

Investment Policy: The fund seeks to provide current income as well as a long-term capital appreciation for its shareholders by investing at least 65% of its total assets in income-producing equity securities primarily.

FAM Equity/Income Investor Fund - FAMEX

800-225-6292
www.famfunds.com

12/29/23   NAV: $53.29   Return: 19.70%

Fenimore Asset Management Trust
384 N. Grand St. – P.O. Box 399
Cobleskill, NY 12043

FUND DETAILS:

Open to all investors

Risk: low

Minimum Investment Purchase: $500

Maximum Front End Sales: no load

Net Expense Ratio: 1.22%

Inception Date: April 1, 1996

Number of Years of Gains: 21

Number of Years of Losses: 6

TOTAL NET ASSETS: $579.73 million

TOP 10 HOLDINGS:

CDW Corporation
Trane Technologies
Arthur J Gallagher & Company
Microchip Technology Incorporated
Ross Stores, Incorporate
Broadridge Financial Solutions, incorporated
Stryker Corporation
Entegris, Incorporated
Republic Services, Incorporated
Paychex, Incorporated

FIVE-YEAR RETURNS:

Year: 2023
Net Asset Value: $53.29 18.87%
Dividend Distribution: $0.37 0.83%
Total Return: 19.70%

Year: 2022
Net Asset Value: $44.83 -14.58%
Dividend Distribution: $.61 1.16%
Total Return: -13.42%

Year: 2021
Net Asset Value: $52.48 23.92%
Dividend Distribution: $.85 2.00%
Total Return: 25.92%

Year: 2020
Net Asset Value: $42.35 10.69%
Dividend Distribution: $0.96 2.51%
Total Return: 13.20%

Year: 2019
Net Asset Value: $38.26 28.69%
Dividend Distribution: $1.13 3.80%
Total Return: 32.49%

MUTUAL FUND RETURNS:

1-year Return: 19.70%
Average Investment: 11.41%
Investment Rank: 10

3-year Return: 10.73%
Average Investment: 9.05%
Investment Rank: 41

5-year Return: 15.58%
Average Investment: 11.11%
Investment Rank: 7

10-year Return: 11.13%
Average Investment: 8.30%
Investment Rank: 2 now

3, 5, and 10-year Return annualized

FLEXIBLE PORTFOLIO

Investment Policy: The fund seeks to maximize total return (capital appreciation plus income) by investing primarily in shares of any number of other no-load and load-waived mutual funds. Over time, the fund's asset mix is likely to consist of a combination of equity, fixed income, or money market funds

.

Teberg Fund -TEBRX
631-470 2621
www.tebergfund.com

12/29/23 NAV: $20.44 Return: 34.92%

Northern Lights Fund Trust III
17605 Wright St.
Omaha, NE 68130

FUND DETAILS:

Open to all investors

Risk: high

Minimum Investment Purchase $2,000

Maximum Front End Sales: no load

Net Expense Ratio: 1.97%

Inception Date: April 1, 2002

Number of Years of Gains: 15

Number of Years of Losses: 6

TOTAL NET ASSETS: $35.6 million

TOP 10 HOLDINGS:

Van Eck Semiconductor ETF
Invesco QQQ Trust
Shares Semiconductor ETF
SPDR Dow Jones Industrial Average ETF Trust
SPDR S&P 500 ETF Trust
BRK.A
Shares Core S&P Small-Cap ETF
Shares Russell 2000 ETF
Financial Select Sector SPDR Fund
Fidelity Low Price Stock

FIVE YEAR RETURNS

Year: 2023
Net Asset Value: $20.44 34.92%
Dividend Distribution: 0.00%
Total Return: 34.92%

Year: 2022
Net Asset Value: $15.15 -22.47%
Dividend Distribution: $0.00
Total Return: -22.47%

Year: 2021
Net Asset Value: $19.54 25.02%
Dividend Distribution: $0.00
Total Return: 25.02%

Year: 2020
Net Asset Value: $15.63 20.05%
Dividend Distribution: $0.07 0.56%
Total Return: 20.61%

Year: 2019
Net Asset Value: $13.02 25.80%
Dividend Distribution: $.08 0.75%
Total Return: 26.55%

MUTUAL FUND RETURNS:

1-year Return: 20.44%
Average Investment: 11.83%
Investment Rank: 3

3-year Return: 12.49%
Average Investment: 2.98%
Investment Rank: 3

5-year Return: 16.93%
Average Investment: 6.72%
Investment Rank: 2

10-year Return: 8.53%
Average Investment: 4.70%
Investment Rank: 4

3, 5, and 10-year Return annualized

GLOBAL GROWTH

Investment policy: The fund seeks to provide shareholders with above average long-term capital growth. Under normal market conditions, at least 80% of the fund's net assets will be invested in equity securities, including companies located in developed and emerging countries.

Columbia Select Global Equity Fund-IGLGX

612-671-4321

www.columbiathreadneedleus.com

12/29/23   NAV: $16.82   Return: 24.47%

Columbia Funds Series Trust II
225 Franklin St.
Boston, MA 02110

FUND DETAILS:

Open to all investors

Risk: above average

Minimum Investment Purchase: $2,000

Maximum Front End Sales: no load

Net Expense Ratio: 1.25%

Inception Date: May 29, 1990

Number of Years of Gains: 23

Number of Years of Losses: 10

TOTAL NET ASSETS: $643.6 million

TOP 10 HOLDINGS:
Microsoft corporation
MasterCard incorporated
Linde PLC
Amazon.Com Incorporated
NVIDIA Corporation
Lam Research Corporation
Alphabet Incorporated
Keyence Corporation
Intuit Incorporated
Synopsys Incorporated

FIVE-YEAR ANNUAL RETURNS:

Year: 2023
Net Asset Value: $16.82 19.12%
Dividend Distribution: $0.76 5.35%
Total Return: 24.47%

Year: 2022
Net Asset Value: $14.12 -28.14%
Dividend Distribution: $0.00
Total Return: -28.14%

Year: 2021
Net Asset Value: $19.65 12.87%
Dividend Distribution: $1.79 10.28%
Total Return: 23.15%

Year: 2020
Net Asset Value: $17.41 16.38%
Dividend Distribution: $1.52 10.18%
Total Return: 26.56%

Year: 2019
Net Asset Value: $14.96 31.00%
Dividend Distribution: $.45 3.93%
Total Return: 34.93%

MUTUAL FUND RETURNS:

1-year Return: 24.47%
Average Investment: 26.73%
Investment Rank: 48

3-year Return: 6.49%
Average Investment: 2.03%
Investment Rank: 29

5-year Return: 16.19%
Average Investment: 12.68%
Investment Rank: 24

10-year Return: 9.60%
Average Investment: 8.84%
Investment Rank: 28

3, 5, and 10-year Return annualized

GLOBAL MULTI-CAP VALUE

Investment policy: The fund seeks long-term capital appreciation by investing principally in equity securities of companies in the gold and precious metals industries.

Vanguard Global Capital Cycles Fund
VGPMX
800-662-2739
www.vanguard.com

12/29/23   NAV: $12.26 Return: 10.03%

Vanguard Group
P.O. Box 2600 - V26
Valley Forge, PA 19482

FUND DETAILS:

Open to all investors

Risk: above average

Minimum Investment Purchase: $3000

Maximum Front End Sales: no load

Net Expense Ratio: 0.36%

Inception Date: May 23, 1984

Number of Years of Gains: 22

Number of Years of Losses: 17

TOTAL NET ASSETS: $1.32 billion

TOP 10 HOLDINGS:

Barrick Gold Corporation
Glencore PLC
American Electric Power Co., Inc.
Samsung electronics Co., Ltd
Intel corporation
Banco Bradesco S.A.
Anglo American PLC
Alibaba Group Holding Limited
Viper Energy, Incorporated
BWX Technologies, Inc.

FIVE-YEAR ANNUAL RETURNS:

Year: 2023
Net Asset Value: $12.26 6.61%
Dividend Distribution: $0.39 3.42%
Total Return: 10.03%

Year: 2022
Net Asset Value: $11.50 3.98%
Dividend Distribution: $0.38 3.41%
Total Return: 7.39%

Year: 2021
Net Asset Value: $11.06 15.69%
Dividend Distribution: $0.36 3.80%
Total Return: 19.49%

Year: 2020
Net Asset Value: $9.56 14.77%
Dividend Distribution: $0.20 2.44%
Total Return: 17.21%

Year: 2019
Net Asset Value: $8.33 18.66%
Dividend Distribution: $0.14 2.00%
Total Return: 20.66%

MUTUAL FUND RETURNS:

1-year Return: 10.06%
Average Investment: 15.44%
Investment Rank: 86

3-year Return: 12.30%
Average Investment: 6.21%
Investment Rank: 3

5-year Return: 14.96%
Average Investment: 10.00%
Investment Rank: 1

10-year Return: 3.87%
Average Investment: 6.31%
Investment Rank: 7

3, 5, and 10-year Return annualized

GLOBAL SMALL/MID-CAP

Investment Policy: The fund seeks long-term growth of capital by investing in U.S. and foreign equity stocks, including common stock, preferred stock, securities convertible into common stock, warrants, rights, and other equity securities having the characteristics of common stock, such as depository receipts.

Kinetics Spin-Off/Corporation Restructuring Fund-LSHAX
800-930-3828
www.kinectics.com

12/29/23 NAV: $18.42 Return: -19.63%

Kinetics Mutual Funds Inc.
555 Taxter Road, Suite 175
Sleepy Hollow, NY 10591

FUND DETAILS:

Open to all investors

Risk: High

Minimum Investment Purchase: $2500

Maximum Front End Sales Load: 5.75%

Net Expense Ratio: 1.63%

Inception Date: May 4, 2007

Number of Years of Gains: 10

Number of Years of Losses: 6

TOTAL NET ASSETS: $23.5 million

TOP 10 HOLDINGS:

Texas Pacific Land Corporation
CSW Industries, Incorporated
Associated Capital Group, Incorporated
GAMCO Investors, Incorporated
Civeo Corporation
Capital Southwest Corporation
Prairie Sky Royalty Limited
Formula One Group
Dream Unlimited Corporation
Howard Hughes Holdings, Inc.

FIVE-YEAR ANNUAL RETURNS:

Year: 2023
Net Asset Value: $18.42 -26.47%
Dividend Distribution: $1.71 6.84%
Total Return: -19.63%

Year: 2022
Net Asset Value: $25.05 37.04%
Dividend Distribution: $0.44 2.41%
Total Return: 39.45%

Year: 2021
Net Asset Value: $18.28 42.59%
Dividend Distribution: $0.02 0.16%
Total Return: 42.75%

Year: 2020
Net Asset Value: $12.82 4.65%
Dividend Distribution: $0.07 0.56%
Total Return: 5.21%

Year: 2019
Net Asset Value: $12.25 32.00%
Dividend Distribution: $0.00
Total Return: 32.00%

MUTUAL FUND RETURNS:

1-year Return: -19.63%
Average Investment: 16.27%
Investment Rank: 98

3-year Return: 20.86%
Average Investment: 1.09%
Investment Rank: 9

5-year Return: 19.96%
Average Investment: 10.14%
Investment Rank: 4

10-year Return: 8.25%
Average Investment: 6.61%
Investment Rank: 12

3, 5, and 10-year Return annualized

LARGE-CAP CORE

Investment Policy: The fund seeks total return greater than the return of the aggregate U.S. stock market as measured by the S&P 500 Index.

Vanguard Growth Income Fund-VQNPX
800-662-2739
www.vanguard.com

12/29/23   NAV: $55.29 Return: 24.32%

The Vanguard Group
PO Box 7800
Philadelphia, PA 19101-9892

FUND DETAILS:

Open to all investors

Risk: Average

Minimum Investment Purchase: $3,000

Maximum Front End Sales Load: no load

Net Expense Ratio: 0.32%

Inception Date: December 10, 1986

Number of Years of Gains: 29

Number of Years of Losses: 8

TOTAL NET ASSETS: $11.6 billion

TOP 10 HOLDINGS

Microsoft Corporation
Apple, Inc
Amazon.com, Inc.
NVIDIA Corporation
Alphabet, Inc.
Visa, Incorporated
Meta Platforms, Incorporated
Merrick & Company, Inc.
Eli Lilly & Company

FIVE-YEAR ANNUAL RETURNS:

Year: 2023
Net Asset Value: $55.29 14.71%
Dividend Distribution: $4.63 9.61%
Total Return: 24.32%

Year: 2022
Net Asset Value: $48.20 -24.57%
Dividend Distribution: $4.67 7.31%
Total Return: -17.26%

Year: 2021
Net Asset Value: $63.90 11.29%
Dividend Distribution: $9.69 16.88%
Total Return: 28.17%

Year: 2020
Net Asset Value: $57.42 10.47%
Dividend Distribution: $3.75 7.21%
Total Return: 17.68%

Year: 2019
Net Asset Value: $51.98 24.41%
Dividend Distribution: $2.13 5.10%
Total Return: 29.51%

MUTUAL FUND RETURNS:

1-year Return: 24.66%
Average Investment: 24.32%
Investment Rank: 55

3-year Return: 11.74%
Average Investment: 8.98%
Investment Rank: 26

5-year Return: 16.48%
Average Investment: 14.80%
Investment Rank: 37

10-year Return: 11.81%
Average Investment: 10.89%
Investment Rank: 20

3, 5, and 10-year Return annualized

LARGE-CAP GROWTH

Investment Policy: The fund seeks to provide investment results that correspond to a benchmark for over-the-calendar securities. The funds current benchmark is the NASDAQ 100 index.

Rydex NASDAQ 100 Fund-RYATX

800-820-0888

www.guggenheiminvestments.com/mutual-funds

12/29/23   NAV: $63.00   Return: 52.95%

Rydex Series Funds
9601 Blackwell Rd. Suite 500
Rockville, MD 20850

FUND DETAILS

Open to all investors

Risk: high

Minimum Investment Purchase: $2,500

Maximum Front End Sales Load: 4.75%

Net Expense Ratio: 1.52%

Inception Date: March 31, 2004

Number of Years of Gains: 16

Number of Years of Losses: 3

TOTAL NET ASSETS: $1.7 billion

TOP 10 HOLDINGS

Microsoft Corporation
Apple, Incorporated
Amazon.com, Inc.
NVIDIA corporation
Broadcom, Inc.
Meda Platforms Inc.
Tesla, Inc.,
Alphabet, Inc.
Costco Wholesale Corporation

FIVE-YEAR ANNUAL RETURNS:

Year: 2023
Net Asset Value: $63.00 52.95%
Dividend Distribution: $0.00 0.00%
Total Return: 52.95%

Year: 2022
Net Asset Value: $41.19   -39.42%
Dividend Distribution: $4.07 5.99%
Total Return: -33.43%

Year: 2021
Net Asset Value: $67.99 19.64%
Dividend Distribution: $3.37 7.81%
Total Return: 27.45%

Year: 2020
Net Asset Value: $56.83 39.77%
Dividend Distribution: $2.61 6.42%
Total Return: 469%

Year: 2019
Net Asset Value: $40.66 34.28%
Dividend Distribution: $0.84 2.77%
Total Return: 37.05%

MUTUAL FUND RETURNS:

1-year Return: 52.95%
Average Investment: 40.53%
Investment Rank: 6

3-year Return: 15.66%
Average Investment: 5.45%
Investment Rank: 15

5-year Return: 26.04%
Average Investment: 16.61%
Investment Rank: 30

10-year Return: 16.12%
Average Investment: 12.64%
Investment Rank: 3

3, 5, and 10-year Return annualized

LARGE-CAP VALUE

Investment Policy: The fund seeks to exceed its benchmark index return. The fund uses derivatives, or combination of derivatives and direct investments, which tracks closely the performance of the index . The fund will also invest in a portfolio of debt se curities to provide additional long-term total return.

DoubleLine Shiller Enhanced Cape N-DSENX
213-633-8200
www.doubleline.com

12/29/23 NAV: $14.26 Return: 26.72%

Double Line Trust
333 South Grand Ave. Suite 1800
Los Angeles, CA 90071

FUND DETAILS:

Open to all investors

Risk: high

Minimum Investment Purchase: $2,000

Maximum Front End Sales Load: no load

Net Expense Ratio: 0.80%

Inception Date: October 31, 2013

Number of Years of Gains: 8

Number of Years of Losses: 2

TOTAL NET ASSETS: $4.1 billion

TOP 10 HOLDINGS

Morgan Stanley Institutional Liquidity Funds

Other 9 holdings unavailable on the Internet. See mutual fund's prospectus.

FIVE-YEAR ANNUAL RETURNS:

Year: 2023
Net Asset Value: $14.26 20.85%
Dividend Distribution: $0.69 5.87%
Total Return: 26.72%

Year: 2022
Net Asset Value: $11.80   -33.67%
Dividend Distribution: $1.90 10.68%
Total Return: -22.99%

Year: 2021
Net Asset Value: $17.79 -3.94%
Dividend Distribution: $5.03 27.16%
Total Return: 23.22%

Year: 2020
Net Asset Value: $18.52 13.89%
Dividend Distribution: $0.28 1.72%
Total Return: 15.61%

Year: 2019
Net Asset Value: $16.26 26.73%
Dividend Distribution: $0.80 6.24%
Total Return: 32.97%

MUTUAL FUND RETURNS:

1-year Return: 26.72%
Average Investment: 13.47%
Investment Rank: 4

3-year Return: 8.98%
Average Investment: 10.21%
Investment Rank: 97

5-year Return: 15.11%
Average Investment: 12.07%
Investment Rank: 24

10-year Return: 12.32%
Average Investment: 8.81%
Investment Rank: 1

3, 5, and 10-year Return annualized

MID-CAP CORE

Investment Policy: The fund seeks long-term capital growth. The fund pursues its investment objective by investing primarily in equity securities of companies with   market capitalizations, at the time of purchase, within the range of companies comprising the Russell Mid-Cap Value index.

Victory Sycamore Established Value Fund-VETAX
800-539-3863
www. investor.vcm.com

12/29/23 NAV: $46.36 Return: 9.95%

Victory portfolios
3435 Stelzer Rd. Suite 1000
Columbus, OH 43219

FUND DETAILS:

Open to all investors

Risk: below average

Minimum Investment Purchase: $2,500

Maximum Front End Sales: 5.75%

Net Expense Ratio: 0.90%

Inception Date: May 5, 2000

Number of Years of Gains: 18

Number of Years of Losses: 5

TOTAL NET ASSETS: $1.41 billion

TOP 10 HOLDINGS

Crown Holdings, Inc.
Quest Diagnostics Incorporated
Textron, Inc.
NNN REIT, Inc.
Leidos Holdings, Inc.
Alliant Energy Corporation
Alexandria Real Estate Equities, Inc.
Lamar Advertising Company
Packaging Corporation of America
Excel Energy

FIVE-YEAR ANNUAL RETURNS:

Year: 2023
Net Asset Value: $46.36 3.71%
Dividend Distribution: $2.79   6.24%
Total Return: 9.95%

Year: 2022
Net Asset Value: $44.70 -9.90%
Dividend Distribution: $3.55 7.16%
Total Return: -2.74%

Year: 2021
Net Asset Value: $49.61 21.33%
Dividend Distribution: $4.02 9.83%
Total Return: 31.16%

Year: 2020
Net Asset Value: $40.89 2.10%
Dividend Distribution: $2.13 5.32%
Total Return: 7.42%

Year: 2019
Net Asset Value: $40.05 22.29%
Dividend Distribution: $2.33 7.11%
Total Return: 29.40%

MUTUAL FUND RETURNS:

1-year Return: 9.95%
Average Investment: 14.71%
Investment Rank: 91

3-year Return: 12.79%
Average Investment: 8.65%
Investment Rank: 10

5-year Return: 14.40%
Average Investment: 12.20%
Investment Rank: 9

10-year Return: 10.67%
Average Investment: 8.10%
Investment Rank: 5

3, 5, and 10-year Return annualized

MID-CAP GROWTH

Investment Policy: The fund seeks long-term growth of capital. Current income is a secondary investment objective The fund invests all net assets in common stocks and is not limited to investments according to a company size.

Value Line Mid-Cap Focused Fund -VLIFX
800-243-2729
www.vlfunds.com

12/29/23 NAV: $32.24 Return: 22.11%

Value Line Funds
P.O. Box 219729
Kansas City, MO 64121-9729

FUND DETAILS:

Open to all investors

Risk: low

Minimum Investment Purchase: $1,000

Maximum Front End Sales: no load

Net Expense Ratio: 1.07%

Inception Date: February 28, 1950

Number of Years of Gains: 57

Number of Years of Losses: 16

TOTAL NET ASSETS: $342 million

TOP 10 HOLDINGS

Gartner, Inc.
CDW Corporation
MSCI, Inc.
Lennox International, Inc.
STERIS PLC
Pool Corporation
TransDigm Group Incorporated
HEICO Corporation
Fair Issac Corporation

FIVE-YEAR ANNUAL RETURNS:

Year: 2023
Net Asset Value: $32.24 22.07%
Dividend Distribution: $0.01 0.04%
Total Return: 22.11%

Year: 2022
Net Asset Value: $26.41 -15.46%
Dividend Distribution: $1.90 6.08%
Total Return: -9.38%

Year: 2021
Net Asset Value: $31.24 10.43%
Dividend Distribution: $2.57 9.08%
Total Return: 19.51%

Year: 2020
Net Asset Value: $28.29 10.98%
Dividend Distribution: $2.21 8.67%
Total Return: 19.65%

Year: 2019
Net Asset Value: $25.49 33.39%
Dividend Distribution: $0.37 1.94%
Total Return: 35.33%

MUTUAL FUND RETURNS:

1-year Return: 22.11%
Average Investment: 21.16 %
Investment Rank: 39

3-year Return: 10.75%
Average Investment:-0.89%
Investment Rank: 2

5-year Return: 17.44%
Average Investment: 12.42%
Investment Rank: 1

10-year Return: 12.80%
Average Investment: 9.23%
Investment Rank: 1

3, 5, and 10-year Return annualized

MID-CAP VALUE

Investment Policy: The fund seeks capital appreciation by investing primarily in common stocks of U.S. companies of all sizes.

Hotchkis & Wiley Mid-Cap Value A-HWMAX
866-493-8637
www. hwcm.com

12/29/23   NAV: $52.61   Return: 19.62%

Hotchkis & Wiley Funds
725 South Figueroa St. - 39th floor
Los Angeles, CA 90017-5439

FUND DETAILS:

Open to all investors

Risk: high

Minimum Investment Purchase: $2,500

Maximum Front End Sales: 5.25%

Net Expense Ratio: 1.21%

Inception Date: January 1, 2001

Number of Years of Gains: 15

Number of Years of Losses: 6

TOTAL NET ASSETS: $116 million

TOP 10 HOLDINGS

Popular, Inc.
Citizens Financial Group, Inc.
Kosmos energy limited
Fluor corporation
Telefonaktiebolaget LM Ericsson (public)
APA corporation
Adient PLC
F5, Inc.
State Street Corporation
Olin Corporation

FIVE-YEAR ANNUAL RETURNS:

Year: 2023
Net Asset Value:$52.61 19.49%
Dividend Distribution: $0.06 0.13%
Total Return: 19.62%

Year: 2022
Net Asset Value: $44.03 1.13%
Dividend Distribution: $0.13 0.29%
Total Return: 1.42%

Year: 2021
Net Asset Value: $43.54 37.31%
Dividend Distribution: $0.52 1.63%
Total Return: 38.94%

Year: 2020
Net Asset Value: $31.71 1.95%
Dividend Distribution: $0.71 2.20%
Total Return: 4.15%

Year: 2019
Net Asset Value: $32.34 11.36%
Dividend Distribution: $0.39 1.33%
Total Return: 12.69%

MUTUAL FUND RETURNS:

1-year Return: 19.62%
Average Investment: 12.40 %
Investment Rank: 7

3-year Return: 19.99%
Average Investment: 11.08%
Investment Rank: 3

5-year Return: 15.36%
Average Investment: 11.53%
Investment Rank: 11%

10-year Return: 6.91%
Average Investment: 7.37%
Investment Rank: 63

3, 5, and 10-year Return annualized

MIXED TARGET ALLOCATION: CONSERVATIVE

Investment policy: The fund seeks high total return with primary emphasis on capital appreciation using a portfolio comprised of 40% stocks, 40% bonds, and 20% money markets.

T. Rowe Price Spectrum Conservative Fund-PRSIX

800-638-5660
www.troweprice.com

12/29/23   NAV: $18.81 Return: 11.96%

T. Rowe Price Funds
100 East Pratt St.
Baltimore, MD 21202

FUND DETAILS:

Open to all investors

Risk: below low average

Minimum Investment Purchase: $2,500

Maximum Front-End Sales: no load

Net Expense Ratio: 0.38%

Inception Date: July 29, 1994

Number of Years of Gains: 25

Number of Years of Losses: 4

TOTAL NET ASSETS: $984.7 million

Top 10 Holdings

T. Rowe Price International Bond Fund USD Hedge
T. Rowe Price Dynamic Global Fund I
T. Rowe Price Institutional Emerging Markets Bond
T. Rowe Price Multi-Strategy Total Return Fund I
T. Rowe Price Institutional High Yield Fund
T. Rowe Price Institutional Emerging Markets Equity
T. Rowe Price Real Assets Fund I
T. Rowe Price U.S. Treasury Long-Tern Index Fund
T. Rowe Price Institutional Floating Rate Fund
Microsoft Corporation

FIVE-YEAR ANNUAL RETURNS:

Year: 2023
Net Asset Value: $18.81 7.73%
Dividend Distribution: $0.74 4.23%
Total Return: 11.96%

Year: 2022
Net Asset Value: $17.46 -18.22%
Dividend Distribution: $0.98 4.59%
Total Return: -13.63%

Year: 2021
Net Asset Value: $21.35 -0.56%
Dividend Distribution: $1.63 7.59%
Total Return: 7.03%

Year: 2020
Net Asset Value: $21.47 7.46% Dividend
Distribution: $0.81 4.05%
Total Return: 11.51%

Year: 2019
Net Asset Value: $19.98 10.88%
Dividend Distribution: $0.74 4.11%
Total Return: 14.99%

MUTUAL FUND RETURNS:
1-year Return: 11.96%
Average Investment: 9.32%
Investment Rank: 7

3-year Return: 1.79%
Average Investment: 0.29%
Investment Rank: 20

5-year Return: 6.37%
Average Investment: 4.38%
Investment Rank: 12

10-year Return: 4.95%
Average Investment: 3.53%
Investment Rank: 3

3, 5, and 10-year Return annualized

MIXED-ASSET: TARGET ALLOCATION GROWTH

Investment Policy: The fund seeks income and capital growth by investing 60% of its assets in stocks and other equity securities and the remainder in bonds and other debt securities, including lower-quality debt securities, when it is outlook is neutral. It invests at least 25% in fixed-income senior securities.

Fidelity Balance Fund – FBALX
800-544-6666
www.fidelity.com

12/29/23   NAV: $26.93   Return: 21.60%

Fidelity Puritan Trust
32 Devonshire Street
Boston, MA 02109

FUND DETAILS:

Open to all investors

Risk: high

Minimum Investment Purchase: N/A

Maximum Front End Sales: no load

Net Expense Ratio: 0.50%

Inception Date: November 6, 1986

Number of Years of Gains: 31

Number of Years of Losses: 6

TOTAL NET ASSETS: $31.07 billion

Top 6 Holdings

Microsoft Corporation
Apple, Inc.3
Amazon.com, Inc.
NVIDIA Corporation
Alphabet Inc.
Meta Platforms, Inc.

FIVE-YEAR ANNUAL RETURNS:

Year: 2023
Net Asset Value: $26.93 17.50%
Dividend Distribution: $.94 4.10%
Total Return: 21.60%

Year: 2022
Net Asset Value: $22.92 -24.53%
Dividend Distribution: $1.85 6.09%
Total Return: -18.44%

Year: 2021
Net Asset Value: $30.37 7.39%
Dividend Distribution: $2.94 10.40%
Total Return: 17.79%

Year: 2020
Net Asset Value: $28.28 14.96%
Dividend Distribution: $1.67 6.79%
Total Return: 21.75%

Year: 2019
Net Asset Value: $24.60 19.13%
Dividend Distribution: $1.04 5.04%
Total Return: 24.17%

MUTUAL FUND RETURNS:

1-year Return: 21.60%
Average Investment: 15.56%
Investment Rank: 5

3-year Return: 6.98%
Average Investment: 4.24%
Investment Rank: 13

5-year Return: 13.37%
Average Investment: 9.14%
Investment Rank: 3

10-year Return: 9.07%
Average Investment: 6.64%
Investment Rank: 3

3, 5, and 10-year Return annualized

MIXED-ASSET: TARGET ALLOCATION MODERATE

Investment Policy: The fund seeks long-term capital growth, consistent with capital preservation and balanced by current income. The fund typically invests 50 to 60% of its assets in equity securities selected primarily for their growth potential and 40-50% in securities chosen primarily for their income potential.

Buffalo Flexible Income Fund - BUFBX
800-492-8332
www.buffalofunds.com

12/29/23 NAV: $19.00 Return: 7.43%

Buffalo funds
c/o U.S. Bank Global Fund Services
PO Box 701
Milwaukee, WI 53201-0701

FUND DETAILS:

Open to all investors

Risk: below average

Minimum Investment Purchase: $2500

Maximum Front End Sales: no load

Net Expense Ratio: 1.01%

Inception Date: August 12, 1994

Number of Years of Gains: 22

Number of Years of Losses: 6

TOTAL NET ASSETS: $337 million

Top 10 Holdings

Microsoft Corporation
Eli Lilly & Company
Hess Corporation
Costco Wholesale Corporation
Conoco Phillips
Chevron Corporation
Exxon Mobile Corporation
Arthur J Gallagher & Company
APA Corporation
PepsiCo, Inc.

FIVE-YEAR ANNUAL RETURNS

Year: 2023
Net Asset Value: $19.00 3.71%
Dividend Distribution: $0.68 3.72%
Total Return: 7.43%

Year: 2022
Net Asset Value: $18.32 -0.16%
Dividend Distribution: $0.77 4.17%
Total Return: 4.01%

Year: 2021
Net Asset Value: $18.35 22.66%
Dividend Distribution: $1.10 7.40%
Total Return: 30.00%

Year: 2020
Net Asset Value: $14.96 -5.56%
Dividend Distribution: $0.53 3.32%
Total Return: -2.24%

Year: 2019
Net Asset Value: $15.84 15.45%
Dividend Distribution: $0.45 3.31%
Total Return: 18.76%

MUTUAL FUND RETURNS:

1-year Return: 7.43%
Average Investment: 12.34%
Investment Rank: 94

3-year Return: 13.81%
Average Investment: 2.63%
Investment Rank: 1

5-year Return: 11.59%
Average Investment: 6.95%
Investment Rank: 2

10-year Return: 7.10%
Average Investment: 5.07%
Investment Rank: 9

3, 5, and 10-year Return annualized

MULTI-CAP CORE

Investment Policy: The fund seeks long-term growth of capital. The fund invests at least 80% of its net assets in equity securities of large capitalization U.S. companies with market capitalizations of less than $3.0 billion. The fund selects stocks that the Sub-Advisor believes yield a more accurate picture of a company's intrinsic value.

Centre American Select Equity -DHAMX
855-298-4236
www. centrefunds.com/dhamx-dhanx

12/29/23 NAV: $15.00 Return: 14.91%

Centre Funds
48 Wall Street
New York, NY 10005

FUND DETAILS:

Open to all investors

Risk: below average

Minimum Investment Purchase: $5000

Maximum Front End Sales: no load

Net Expense Ratio: 1.46%

Inception Date: December 21, 2011

Number of Years of Gains: 10

Number of Years of Losses: 1

TOTAL NET ASSETS: $269.9 million

Top 10 Holdings

Apple, Inc.
Microsoft Corporation
Amazon.com, Inc.
Johnson & Johnson
NVIDIA Corporation
PepsiCo, Inc.
Medtronic PLC
Zimmer Biomet Holdings Inc
Altria Group, Inc.
F5, Inc.

FIVE YEAR ANNUAL RETURNS:

Year: 2023
Net Asset Value: $15.00 12.02%
Dividend Distribution: $0.39 2.89%
Total Return: 14.91%

Year: 2022
Net Asset Value: $13.39 -4.63%
Dividend Distribution: $0.19 1.32%
Total Return: -3.31%

Year: 2021
Net Asset Value: $14.04 9.69%
Dividend Distribution: $2.27 17.70%
Total Return: 27.39%

Year: 2020
Net Asset Value: $12.80 25.12% Dividend
Distribution: $0.58 5.66%
Total Return: 30.78%

Year: 2019
Net Asset Value: $10.23 5.90%
Dividend Distribution: $1.02 10.54%
Total Return: 16.44%

MUTUAL FUND RETURNS:

1-year Return: 14.91%
Average Investment: 21.27%
Investment Rank: 4

3-year Return: 13.00%
Average Investment: 7.43%
Investment Rank: 4

5-year Return: 17.24%
Average Investment: 13.48%
Investment Rank: 7

10-year Return: 11.55%
Average Investment: 9.62%
Investment Rank: 11

3, 5, and 10-year Return annualized

MULTI-CAP GROWTH

Investment Policy: The fund seeks long-term capital appreciation through investment in companies believed to be selling below intrinsic value. The price of shares in relation to book value, asset value, earnings, dividends, and cash flow.

Schwartz Value Focus Fund – RCMFX

888-726 0753
www.schwartzinvest.com

12/29/23 NAV: $43.73 Return: 1.18%

Schwartz Value Focused Fund
c/o Ultimus Fund Solutions, LLC
135 Merchant St., Suite 230
Cincinnati, OH 45246

FUND DETAILS:

Open to all investors

Risk: high

Minimum Investment Purchase: $2,500

Maximum Front End Sales: no load

Net Expense Ratio: 1.25%

Inception Date: July 20, 1993

Number of Years of Gains: 30

Number of Years of Losses: 10

TOTAL NET ASSETS: $51.7 million

Top 10 Holdings

Texas Pacific Land Corporation
The St. Joe Company
Pioneer Natural Resources Company
MasterCard, Incorporated
Masco Corporation
Moody's Corporation
Schlumberger limited
Intercontinental Exchange, Inc.
Madison Square Garden sports corporation
BRK.A

FIVE-YEAR ANNUAL RETURNS:

Year: 2023
Net Asset Value: $43.73 -1.33%
Dividend Distribution: $1.13 2.51%
Total Return: 1.18%

 Year: 2022
Net Asset Value: $45.06 20.10%
Dividend Distribution: $0.39 1.05%
Total Return: 21.15%

Year: 2021
Net Asset Value: $37.52 22.86%
Dividend Distribution: $2.53 8.28%
Total Return: 31.14%

Year: 2020
Net Asset Value: $30.54 8.95%
Dividend Distribution: $0.75 2.67%
Total Return: 11.62%

Year: 2019
Net Asset Value: $28.03 18.67%
Dividend Distribution: $0
Total Return: 18.67%

MUTUAL FUND RETURNS:

1-year Return: 1.18%
Average Investment: 32.89%
Investment Rank: 100

3-year Return: 17.82%
Average Investment: 0.01%
Investment Rank: 1

5-year Return: 16.75%
Average Investment: 12.41%
Investment Rank: 25

10-year Return: 7.79%
Average Investment: 10.87%
Investment Rank: 90%

3, 5, and 10-year Return annualized

MULTI-CAP VALUE

Investment Policy: The Fund seeks long-term capital appreciation predicted on the belief that, overtime, market price and value converge, and that investment in securities price significantly below long-term value presents the best opportunity to achieve this objective.

Oakmark Fund, Investor - OAKMX
800-625-6275
www.oakmark.com

12/29/23 NAV: $132.56 Return: 30.89%

Harris Associates LP
111 South Wacker Drive - Suite 4600
Chicago, IL 60606

FUND DETAILS:

Open to all investors
Risk: average
Minimum Investment Purchase: $1000
Maximum Front End Sales: No load
Net Expense Ratio: 0.89%

Inception Date: August 5, 1991

Number of Years of Gains: 24

Number of Years of Losses: 8

TOTAL NET ASSETS: $19.1 billion

Top 9 Holdings

Capital One Financial Corporation
Intercontinental Exchange, Inc.
Wells Fargo& company
Conoco Phillips
KKR & Company, Inc.
IQVIA Holdings, Inc.
Comcast Corporation
American International Group, Inc.
Fiserv, In

FIVE YEAR ANNUAL RETURNS:

Year: 2023
Net Asset Value: $132.56 29.57%
Dividend Distribution: $1.35 %1.32%
Total Return: 30.89%

Year: 2022
Net Asset Value: $102.31 -14.15%
Dividend Distribution: $.94 0.79%
Total Return: -13.36%

Year: 2021
Net Asset Value: $119.17 26.47%
Dividend Distribution: $1.75 1.86%
Total Return: 28.33%

Year: 2020
Net Asset Value: $94.23 17.85%
Dividend Distribution: $0.15 0.19%
Total Return: 18.04%

Year 2019
Net Asset Value: $79.96 17.09%
Dividend Distribution: $6.66 9.75%
Total Return: 26.84%

MUTUAL FUND RETURNS:

1-year Return: 30.89%
Average Investment: 12.37%
Investment Rank: 3

3-year Return: 15.29%
Average Investment: 10.17%
Investment Rank: 4

5-year Return: 18.15%
Average Investment: 11.54%
Investment Rank: 2

10-year Return: 11.36%
Average Investment: 8.08%
Investment Rank: 2

3, 5, and 10-year Return annualized

SECTOR: FINANCIAL INSURANCE

Investment Policy: The fund seeks capital appreciation. The fund invests at least 80% of the assets in the securities of companies principally engaged in under writing, reinsuring, selling, distributing, or placing property and casualty, life, or health insurance, while using fundamental analysis of factors in selecting investment

Fidelity Select Insurance Portfolio -FSPCX
877-208-0098
www.fidelity.com

12/29/23   NAV: $76.67 Return: 12.98%

Fidelity Select Portfolios
82 Devonshire Street
Boston, MA 02109

FUND DETAILS:

Open to all investors

Risk: average

Minimum Investment Purchase: NA

Maximum Front End Sales: no load

Net Expense Ratio: 0.73%

Inception Date: June 30, 1986

Number of Years of Gains: 29

Number of Years of Losses: 8

TOTAL NET ASSETS: $1.55 billion

Top 10 Holdings

Marsh & McLennan companies, Inc.
Chubb Limited
The Travelers Companies, Inc.
The Hartford Financial Services Group, Inc.
Arthur J Gallagher & Co.
The Allstate Corporation
American Financial Group, Inc
Unum Group
Reinsurance Group of America, Inc.
Corebridge Financial, Inc.

FIVE-YEAR RETURNS:

Year: 2023
Net Asset Value: $76.67 3.54%
Dividend Distribution: $6.99 9.44%
Total Return: 12.98%

Year: 2022
Net Asset Value: $74.05 6.95%
Dividend Distribution: $0.56 0.81%
Total Return: 7.76%

Year: 2021
Net Asset Value: $69.24 18.43%
Dividend Distribution: $6.34 10.87%
Total Return: 29.30%

Year: 2020
Net Asset Value: $58.46 -9.60%
Dividend Distribution: $6.07 9.38%
Total Return: -0.22%

Year: 2019
Net Asset Value: $64.67 22.48%
Dividend Distribution: $3.99 7.55%
Total Return: 30.03%

MUTUAL FUND RETURNS:

1-year Return: 12.98%
Average Investment: 10.96%
Investment Rank: 50

3-year Return: 16.68%
Average Investment: 7.76%
Investment Rank: 2

5-year Return: 15.97%
Average Investment: 9.58%
Investment Rank: 5

10-year Return: 10.93%
Average Investment: 7.15%
Investment Rank: 5

3, 5, and 10-year Return annualized

SECTOR: HEALTH /BIOTECHNOLOGY

Investment Policy: The fund seeks capital appreciation. Under normal market conditions, the fund invests at least 80% of assets in securities of companies principally engaged in the ownership or management of hospitals, nursing homes, health maintenance organizations, and other companies specializing in the delivery of health care services

Fidelity Select Health Care Services-FSHCX
877-208-0098
www.fidelity.com

12/29/23 NAV: $133.22 Return: 1.51%

Fidelity Select Portfolios
82 Devonshire St.
Boston, MA 02/1/09

FUND DETAILS:

Open to all investors
T
Risk: average

Minimum Investment Purchase: N/A

Maximum Front End Sales: no load

Net Expense Ratio: 0.73%

Inception Date: June 30, 1986

Number of Years of Gains: 29

Number of Years of Losses: 8

TOTAL NET ASSETS: $1.55 billion

Top 10 Holdings

United Health Group, Inc.
CVS Health Corporation
The Cigna Group
Centene Corporation
Cencora, Inc.
Molina Healthcare, Inc
HCA Healthcare, Inc.
Mc Kesson Corporation
Elevance Health, Inc.
Acadia Healthcare Company, Inc

FIVE-YEAR ANNUAL RETURNS:

Year: 2023
Net Asset Value: $133.22 0.92%
Dividend Distribution: $0.78 0.59%
Total Return: 1.51%

Year: 2022
Net Asset Value: $132.00 -4.06%
Dividend Distribution: $7.02 5.10%
Total Return: 1.04%

Year: 2021
Net Asset Value: $137.58 11.74 percent
Dividend Distribution: $9.76 7.93%
Total Return: 19.67%

Year: 2020
Net Asset Value: $123.12 17.40%
Dividend Distribution: $0.93 0.89%
Total Return: 18.29%

Year: 2019
Net Asset Value: $104.87 19.58%
Dividend Distribution: $0.29 0.33%
Total Return: 19.91%

MUTUAL FUND RETURNS:

1-year Return: 1.51%
Average Investment: 4.65%
Investment Rank: 29

3-year Return: 7.41%
Average Investment: -0.84%
Investment Rank: 2

5-year Return: 12.08%
Average Investment: 9.29%
Investment Rank: 9

10-year Return: 12.53%
Average Investment: 9.09%
Investment Rank: 4

3, 5, and 10-year Return annualized

SECTOR: S&P 500 INDEX

Investment Policy: The Fund seeks to provide investment results that correspond to the total performance of common stocks publicly traded in the United States. It invests in common stocks that are in the S&P 500 index, a widely recognized, unmanaged index of common stock prices, and broadly represents the performance of common stocks.

Fidelity 500 Index Fund -FXAIX

877-208-0098

www.fidelity.com

12/29/23 NAV: $165.49 Return: 26.29%

Fidelity Select Portfolio
82 Devonshire St.
Boston, MA 02109

FUND DETAILS:

Open to all investors

Risk: average
Minimum Investment Purchase: N/A

Maximum Front-End Sales: no load

Net Expense Ratio: 0.12%

Inception Date: May 4, 2011

Number of Years of Gains: 10

Number of Years of Losses: 2

TOTAL NET ASSETS: $407.6 billion

Top 10 Holdings

Apple, Inc.
Microsoft Corporation
Amazon.com, Inc.
NVIDIA Corporation
Alphabet, Inc.
Meta Platforms, Inc.
Alphabet, Inc.
Tesla, Inc.
Berkshire Hathaway, Inc
J P Morgan Chase & Company

FIVE YEAR ANNUAL RETURNS:

Year: 2023
Net Asset Value: $165.49 24.32%
Dividend Distribution: $2.62 1.97%
Total Return: 26.29%

Year: 2022
Net Asset Value: $133.12 -19.48%
Dividend Distribution: $2.26 1.37%
Total Return: -18.11%

Year: 2021
Net Asset Value: $165.32 27.00%
Dividend Distribution: $2.02 1.55%
Total Return: 28.55%

Year: 2020
Net Asset Value: $130.17 16.20%
Dividend Distribution: $2.08 1.86%
Total Return: 18.06%

Year: 2019
Net Asset Value: $112.02 28.61%
Dividend Distribution: $2.31 2.65%
Total Return: 31.26%

MUTUAL FUND RETURNS:

1-year Return: 26.29%
Average Investment: 25.34%
Investment Rank: 6

3-year Return: 12.24%
Average Investment: 9.78%
Investment Rank: 2

5-year Return: 17.21%
Average Investment: 15.35%
Investment Rank: 5

10-year Return: 12.05%
Average Investment: 11.54%
Investment Rank: 2

3, 5, and 10-year Return annualized

SECTOR: SCIENCE & TECHNOLOGY

Investment Policy: The Fund seeks capital appreciation by investing primarily in companies engaged in the design, manufacture, or sale of electronic components (semiconductors, printed circuit boards, and other components) karma equipment vendors, component distributors, inventors of instruments and electronic systems

Fidelity Select Semiconductors Portfolio-FSELX

877-208-0098
www.fidelity.com

12/29/23 NAV: $24.25 Return: 78.14%

Fidelity Investments
P.O. Box 5000
Cincinnati, OH 45273-8610

FUND DETAILS:

Open to all investors
Risk: high
Minimum Investment Purchase: NA
Maximum Front End Sales: no load
Net Expense Ratio: 0.69%

Inception Date: July 29, 1985

Number of Years of Gains: 27

Number of Years of Losses: 11

TOTAL NET ASSETS: $9.50 billion

Top10 Holdings

NVIDIA Corporation
NXP Semiconductors N.V.
ON Semiconductor Corporation
Marvel Technology Inc.
GlobalFoundries, Inc.
Broadcom, Inc.
Taiwan Semiconductor Manufacturing Company Ltd
Micron Technology, Inc.
ASML Holden, Inc.
Lam Research Corporation

FIVE YEAR ANNUAL RETURNS:

Year: 2023
Net Asset Value: $24.25 65.98%
Dividend Distribution: $1.78 12.16%
Total Return: 78.14%

Year: 2022
Net Asset Value: $14.61 -38.72%
Dividend Distribution: $0.98 4.11%
Total Return: -34.61%

Year: 2021
Net Asset Value: $23.84 46.98%
Dividend Distribution: $1.67 10.30%
Total Return: 57.28%

Year: 2020
Net Asset Value: $16.22 29.55%
Dividend Distribution: $1.32 10.54%
Total Return: 40.09%

Year: 2019
Net Asset Value: $12.52 59.09%
Dividend Distribution: $0.43 5.46%
Total Return: 64.55%

MUTUAL FUND RETURNS:

1-year Return: 63.03%

average category: 46.06%

investment rank: 8%

3-year Return: 33.60%

average category: 14.96%

investment rank: 22%

5-year Return: 41.09%

average category: 2.92%

investment rank: 27%

10-year Return: 4.94%

average category: 7%

investment rank: 22%

3, 5, and 10-year Return annualized

SECTOR: TELECOMMUNICATION

Investment Policy: The Fund seeks to provide long-term capital growth. It invests primarily in common stocks of companies operating in the media, telecommunications, and technology industries, such as entertainment, broadcasting, and advanced communications networks.

T. Rowe Price Communication & Technology Fund-PRMTX
800-225-5132
www.troweprice.com

12/29/23 NAV: $119.52 Return: 39.28%

T. Rowe Price Media & Telecommunication
100 E Pratt St.
Baltimore, MD 21202

FUND DETAILS:

Open to all investors
Risk: average
Minimum Investment Purchase: $2,500
Maximum Front End Sales: no load
Net Expense Ratio: 0.77%
Inception Date: October 13, 1993

Number of Years of Gains: 22

Number of Years of Losses: 8

TOTAL NET ASSETS: $4.09 billion

Top 10 Holdings

Meta Platforms, Inc.
Alphabet, Inc.
Microsoft corporation
T-Mobile U.S., Inc.
Netflix, Inc.
Amazon. com, Inc.
Apple, Inc.
NVIDIA Corporation
Verizon Communications Inc.
Booking Holdings, Inc.

FIVE YEAR ANNUAL RETURNS:

Year: 2023
Net Asset Value: $119.52 29.15%
Dividend Distribution: $9.37 10.13%
Total Return: 39.28%

Year: 2022
Net Asset Value: $92.54 -49.32%
Dividend Distribution: $16.20 8.87%
Total Return: -40.45%

Year: 2021
Net Asset Value: $182.60 1.17%
Dividend Distribution: $15.25 8.45%
Total Return: 9.62%

Year: 2020
Net Asset Value: $180.49
Dividend Distribution: $9.55 7.72%
Total Return: 53.56%

Year: 2019
Net Asset Value: $123.76 32.28%
Dividend Distribution: $1.52 1.62%
Total Return: 33.90%

MUTUAL FUND RETURNS:

1-year Return: 39.28%
Average Investment: 23.21%
Investment Rank: 32

3-year Return: 2.82%
Average Investment: -2.41%
Investment Rank: 42

5-year Return: 19.18%
Average Investment: 6.74%
Investment Rank: 16

10-year Return: 11.90%
Average Investment: 4.54%
Investment Rank: 7

3, 5, and 10-year Return annualized

SMALL-CAP CORE

Investment Policy: The Fund seeks to provide long-term capital appreciation. The fund seeks to use a multi- cap strategy without regard to whether the securities are conventionally categorized as large, mid, small, or micro-cap; or whether they are categorized as growth or value stocks.

Auer Growth Fund - AUERX
888-711-2837
www.sbauerfunds.com

12/29/23 NAV: $14.82 Return: 26.29%

Auer Growth Fund
Unified Series Trust
2960 N. Meridian Street, Suite 300
Indianapolis, IN 46208

FUND DETAILS:

Open to all investors

Risk: above average

Minimum Investment Purchase: $2,000

Maximum Front End Sales: no load

Net Expense Ratio: 2.37%

Inception Date: December 28, 2007

Number of Years of Gains: 10

Number of Years of Losses: 6

TOTAL NET ASSETS: $41.70 million

Top 10 Holdings

Fidelity Colchester Street Trust
Government Portfolio
Euroseas, Ltd
Phillips 66
PBF Energy, Inc.
Heister-Yale Materials Handling, Inc.
General Motors company
Tidewater, Inc.
Forestar Group, Inc.
ANI Pharmaceuticals, Inc.

FIVE YEAR ANNUAL RETURNS:

Year: 2023
Net Asset Value: $14.82 15.78%
Dividend Distribution: $0.70 5.51%
Total Return: 21.29%

Year: 2022
Net Asset Value: $12.80   3.90%
Dividend Distribution: $.75 6.07%
Total Return: 9.97%

Year: 2021
Net Asset Value: $12.32   45.11%
Dividend Distribution: $0.00
Total Return: 45.11%

Year: 2020
Net Asset Value: $8.49   -1.85%
Dividend Distribution: $0.00
Total Return: -1.85%

Year: 2019
Net Asset Value: $8.65 27.96%
Dividend Distribution: $0.00
Total Return: 27.96%

MUTUAL FUND RETURNS:

1-year Return: 21.29%

average category: 15.57%

investment rank: 10

3-years Return: 25.46%

average category: 7.58%

investment rank: 1

5-years Return: 20.50%

average category: 11.00%

investment rank: 1

10-years Return: 6.78%

average category: 7.13%

investment rank: 64

3, 5, and 10-year Return annualized

SMALL-CAP GROWTH

Investment category: the fund 6 long term capital appreciation, with dividend income as a secondary consideration. This fund invests primarily in equity securities, usually common stocks of small and mid-capitalization domestic companies-

Virtus KAR Small-Cap Fund – PKSAX
800-243 1574
www.virtus.com

12/29/23 NAV: $47.83 Return: 32.00%

Virtus Equity Trust
101 Munson St.
Greenfield, MA 01301

FUND DETAILS:

Open to all investors

Risk: low

Minimum Investment Purchase: $2500

Maximum Front End Sales: 5.50%

Net Expense Ratio: 1.27%

Inception Date: August 30, 2002

Number of Years of Gains: 17

Number of Years of Losses: 4

TOTAL NET ASSETS: $141.80 million

TOP 10 HOLDINGS

Simpson Manufacturing Company, Inc.
EMCOR, Group, Inc.
FTI Consulting, Inc.
Primerica, Inc.
Manhattan Associates, Inc.
Acushnet holdings corporation
CorVel Corporation
The Toro Company
Watts Water Technologies Inc.
Landstar System, Inc

FIVE YEAR ANNUAL RETURNS:

Year: 2023
Net Asset Value: $47.83 26.40%
Dividend Distribution: $2.12 5.60%
Total Return: 32.00%

Year: 2022
Net Asset Value: $37.84 -15.91%
Dividend Distribution: $2.68 5.88%
Total Return: -10.03%

Year: 2021
Net Asset Value: $45.54 4.81%
Dividend Distribution: $5.84 13.44%
Total Return: 18.25%

Year: 2020
Net Asset Value: $43.45 10.84%
Dividend Distribution: $3.39 8.75%
Total Return: 19.59%

Year: 2019
Net Asset Value: $38.74 34.09%
Dividend Distribution: $1.65 5.71%
Total Return: 39.80%

MUTUAL FUND RETURNS:

1-year Return: 47.83%
average category: 32.00%
investment rank: 3

3-years Return: 13.41%
average category: -2.17%
investment rank: 1

5-years Return: 19.92%
average category: 10.97%
investment rank: 2

10-years Return: 14.54%
average category: 7.99%
investment rank: 1

3, 5, and 10-year Return annualized

SMALL-CAP VALUE

Investment Policy: The Fund seeks to provide long-term total Return of capital, primarily through capital appreciation. The Fund invest in a diversified portfolio of small stocks. Bridgeway Funds define small stocks as companies that are smaller than the largest 500 U.S. companies as measured by market capitalization.

Invesco Small-Cap Value Fund- VSCAX
800-959-4246
www.invesco.com

12/29/23 NAV: $20.31 Return: 22.91%

Aim Sector Funds
11 Greenway Plaza, Suite 100
Houston, TX 77046

FUND DETAILS:

Open to all investors

Risk: high

Minimum Investment Purchase: $1000

Maximum Front-End Sales: 5.50%

Net Expense Ratio: 1.09%

Inception Date: June 21, 1999

Number of Years of Gains: 17

Number of Years of Losses: 6

TOTAL NET ASSETS: $2.6 billion

TOP 10 HOLDINGS:

Lumentum Holdings, Inc.
Coherent Corporation
Expedia Group, Inc.
Western Alliance Bancorporation
Pinnacle Financial Partners, Inc.
Vertiv Holdings Company
Huntington Bancshares, Inc.
Webster Financial Corporation
NRG, Inc.
Leonardo S.p.a.

FIVE-YEAR ANNUAL RETURNS:

Year: 2023
Net Asset Value: $20.31 16.99%
Dividend Distribution: $1.02 5.92%
Total Return: 22.91%

Year: 2022
Net Asset Value: $17.36   -5.45%
Dividend Distribution: $1.79   9.77%
Total Return: 4.32%

Year: 2021
Net Asset Value $18.36 15.98%
Dividend Distribution: $3.25 20.53%
Total Return: 36.51%

Year: 2020
Net Asset Value: $15.83 10.47%
Dividend Distribution: $0.05 0.34%
Total Return: 10.81%

Year: 2019
Net Asset Value: $14.33 21.13%
Dividend Distribution: $1.29 10.92%
Total Return: 32.05%

MUTUAL FUND RETURNS:

1-year Return: 22.91%
average category: 16.34%
investment rank: 11

3-years Return: 21.25%
average category: 12.51%
investment rank: 3

5-years Return: 21.32%
average category: 12.08%
investment rank: 3

10-years Return: 10.12%
average category: 6.57%
investment rank: 3

3, 5, and 10-year Return annualized

Self-Directed Retirement Investing

If you are a wage earner, middle-aged or older, invest in one of the best types of investment portfolios (Individual Retirement Account) to build a prosperous nest egg. It is essential to plan and be prepared for retirement today, not tomorrow.   This can best be achieved by establishing a goal, committing to the goal, and persevering.

1. Establishing Goal: You, the investor of a mutual fund, must determine which goal in your investment would best achieve the financial return for you.

2. Aggressive goals are methods to achieve maximum returns. An aggressive investment strategy attempts to grow assets above average compared to its industry or the overall market.

3.   Conservative goals are investment strategies that grow capital over the long-term. This type of fund has a minimal asset turno v e r or a high

Percentage of fixed assets and use a buy-hold investment strategy.

Moderate goals are investments that attempt to reduce risks and increase returns equally. The investment may incur a short-term loss of principal. And the lower degree of liquidity in exchange for long-term appreciation.

Perseverance: It is difficult to save money, especially when encountering tough times. You, the investor, should make every effort to save money, even under these conditions. Once the crisis no longer exists, continue investing as planned.

Commitment: To attain your financial goals, you must commit to the money saved and invested in your retirement portfolio. After making the minimum investment and being a shareholder of the mutual fund, you can always make additional purchases.

Every year the maximum investment you can

contribute to your traditional IRA and Roth IRA is $6,500 for individuals under the age of 50. The maximum investment is $7,500 for individuals 50 years of age or older.

To maximize your annual performance be sure to reinvest all distribution received every year!

Maximizing Retirement/Savings Wealth

Here is a factual investment illustrating how to accumulate retirement wealth. The model covers 2010 through 2023. Acquiring this financial success, demand commitment in making maximum annual IRA investments and reinvesting all distributions.

Mutual Fund: Oakmark I–OAKMX

Investment Category: Multi-Cap Core

June 1, 2010
IRA Purchase: $6,000
Net Asset Value: $36.91
Total Shares Purchased: 162.5576

December 17, 2010
Distribution: $0.25 $40 $0.64
Shares Reinvested 1.0098
Total Shares Owned 163.5674

December 31, 2010

Net Asset Value: $41.30

Total Shares Owned: 163.5674

June 1, 2011

IRA Purchase: $6,000

Net Asset Value: $43.74

Total Shares Purchased: 137.1742

December 19, 2011
Distribution: $.35 $105.26
Shares Reinvested: 2.6341
Total Shares Owned: 303.3757

December 30, 2011
Net Asset Value: $41.69
Total Shares Owned: 303.3757
Portfolio Value: $12,647.73 5.40%

June 1, 2012
IRA Purchase: $6,000
Net Asset Value: $42.86
Total Shares Purchased: 140.0887

December 18, 2012

Distribution: $1.88 $903.12

Shares Reinvested: 19.3595

Total Shares Owned: 462.8239

December 31, 2012

Net Asset Value: $48.53

Total Shares Owned: 462.8239

IRA Portfolio Value: $22,460.84

June 1, 2013

IRA Purchased: $6,500

Net Asset Value: $57.16

Total Shares Purchased: 113.716

December 19, 2013

Distribution: $3.00 $1,840

Shares Reinvested: 27.1138

Total Shares Owned: 603.6536

December 31, 2013

Net Asset Value: $62.09

Total Shares Owned: 603.653

IRA Portfolio Value: $37,480.85

June 1, 2014

IRA Purchase: $6,500

Net Asset Value: $66.67

Total Shares Purchased: 97.4951

December 18, 2014

Distribution: $4.55 $3,190

Shares Reinvested: 48.2636

Total Shares Owned: 749.4123

December 31, 2014

Net Asset Value: $66.38

Total Shares Owned: 749.4123

IRA Portfolio Value: $49,745.99

June 1, 2015

IRA Purchase: $6,500

Net Asset Value: $67.66

Total Shares Purchased: 96.0686

December 17, 2015

Distribution: $.90 $760.93

Shares Reinvested: 12.1148

Total Shares Owned: 857.5957

December 31, 2015

Net Asset Value: $62.86

Total Shares Owned: 857.5957

IRA Portfolio Value: $53,908.47

June 1, 2016

IRA Purchase: $6,500

Net Asset Value: $64.88

Total Shares Purchased: 100.1850

November 28, 2016

Distribution: $1.87 $1603

Shares Reinvested: 22.7250

Total Shares Owned: 980.5057

December 30, 2016

Net Asset Value: $72.48

Total Shares Owned: 980.5057

IRA Portfolio Value: $71,067.05

June 1, 2017

IRA Purchase: $6,500

Net Asset Value: $78.58

Total Shares Purchased: 82.7182

December 14, 2017

Distribution: $3.42

Shares Reinvested: 46.87

Total Shares Owned: 1110.09

December 29, 2017

Net Asset Value: $84.33

Total Shares Owned: 1110.09

IRA Portfolio Value: $93,614.22

June 1, 2018

IRA Purchase: $6,500

Net Asset Value: $85.37

Total Shares Purchased: 76.1392

December 13, 2018

Distribution: $5.55 $658

Shares Reinvested: $71.50

Total Shares Owned: 1278.3071

December 29, 2018

Net Asset Value: $68.29

Total Shares Owned: 1278.3071

IRA Portfolio Value: $87,295.59

June 3, 2019

IRA Purchase: $6,500

Net Asset Value: $73.60

Total Shares Purchased: 88.3152

December 12, 2019

Distribution: $6.66

Shares Reinvested: 115.4306

Total Shares Owned: 1482.0529

December 31, 2019

Net Asset Value: $79.96

Total Shares Owned: 1482.0529

IRA Portfolio Value: $118,504.95

June 18, 2020

IRA Purchase: $6,500

Net Asset Value: $68.51

Total Shares Purchased: 94.8766

December 10, 2020

Net Asset Value $88.85

Distribution: $.15 $236.54

Shares Reinvested: 2.6622

December 31, 2020

Net Asset Value: $94.23

Total Shares Owned: 1579.5917

IRA Portfolio: $148,844.92

The last investment purchased was June 18, 2020, no additional investments were purchased! Each year thereafter, shares of investments were acquired by "reinvesting all distribution" of income and capital gains.

December 16, 2021

Net Asset Value: $119.17

Distribution: $1.75 Shares Reinvested: 23.4823

Total Shares Owned: 1603.074

December 31, 2021

Net Asset Value: $119.17

Total Shares Owned: 1603.074

December 16, 2022

Net Asset Value: $102.56

Distribution: $.94   Shares Reinvested: 14.697

Total Shares Owned: 1617.771

December 30, 2022

Net Asset Value: $102.31

Total Shares Owned: 1617.771

IRA Portfolio: $165,514.18

December 4, 2023

Net Asset Value: $131.83

Distribution: $1.35 Shares Reinvested: 16.554

Total Shares Owned: 1634.325

December 29, 2023

Net Asset Value: $132.56

Total Shares Owned: 1634.325

Value IRA Portfolio: $216,646.12

December 29, 2023 Investment Prosperity:

IRA Investments: $70,000 (2010 thru 2020)

Reinvestment: $146,646.12 2010 thru 2023

Total IRA Portfolio Value: $216,646.12

Return: 16.11%

An individual Retirement Account (IRA) is one of the best investments available when planning for retirement. As an owner of IRA accounts, you make all the decisions on the investment's success or failure. You manage and control the assets in the investment. You decide if the investment will be aggressive, moderate, or conservative. You determine the amount of money to be invested and how often. Most important, you select the moneymaking investment that will most profitable.

Traditional IRAs are a terrific way to save for the future! All reinvested mutual fund income and capital gains distribution are not taxable until you reach the age of 73. Go to the Internal Revenue Service guidelines:

https://www.irs.gov/retirement-plans/traditional-and-roth-iras

Starting 2024, the maximum Traditional and Roth IRA purchase is $6,500 for individuals under 50 years of age or $7,500 if you are age 50 or older by the end of the year.

IRS Withholding Calculator: this helps to determine federal income tax withholding so your employer can withhold the correct amount from your salary. This is especially helpful if you are starting a new job.

IRA Contribution at age 73: You cannot make contributions to traditional IRA investments. However, you can still contribute to a Roth IRA and make rollover contributions to a Roth IRA.

Required Minimum Distribution: The IRS requires that you take the mutual fund distribution once you reach the age of 73. You may be subject to a 50% non-deductible federal excise tax. Tax Exempt: Investment income or capital gain distributions reinvested are tax exempt until 73 years of age.

The Investor Government Required Minimum $6,500 persons under 50 years of age, or $7,500 if you are age 50 or older by the end of the year, or your Taxable compensation for the year.

IRS Withholding Calculator: This helps in determine federal income tax withholding so your employer can withhold the correct amount from your salary. This is especially helpful if you are starting a new job.

IRA Contribution at age 73: You cannot make contributions to traditional IRA investments. However, you can still contribute to a Roth IRA and make rollover contributions to a Roth IRA.

Required Minimum Distribution: The IRS requires that you take the mutual fund distribution once you reach the age of 73. You may be subject to a 50% non-deductible federal excise tax. Tax Exempt: Investment income or capital gain distributions reinvested are tax exempt until 73 years of age.

The Investor Government Required Minimum Distribution calculator determines the total dollar amount that must be withdrawn for the taxable year. Investors are not required to withdraw money from any one specific IRA investment account. It can be a combined total

Withdrawal from several IRA investments making certain the total Required Minimum Distribution withdrawals taken are required minimum for that year. Any minimum amount of withdraw that is short of the RMD is subject to severe tax liability.

Retirement planning: select mutual fund investments that provide consistent above-average performance. You should make mutual fund investments right at the top in the investment category. Making sure that most years of performance have more return gains and fewer return losses. Deciding the type of risk, low risk, average-risk, moderate-risk, or high-risk, will best achieve your financial goals. Mutual fund investments can be purchased directly from the mutual fund or from a financial advisor.

Reference Source of Information:

Wall Street Journal
https://www.wsj.com/market-data/quotes

MORNINGSTAR
https://www.morningstar.com/funds

BARRON'S
https://www.barrons.com/market-data/funds

Yahoo! Finance
https://finance.yahoo.com/quote

Big Charts
https://bigcharts.marketwatch.com/historical

Individual Requirement Arrangements
https://www.irs.gov

Traditional IRAs/IRS
https://www.irs.gov/retirement-plans/

About the Author:

King A. Kovacs (Mutual Fund Analyst, Researcher & Author) founder of Mutual Interest Data Service, Ltd. in 1999 to find moneymakers for mutual fund investments the author extensively researched and analyzed thousands of mutual funds every year. The result is the author identified 29 profit making mutual funds. Each fund is categorized according to investment objectives which allows investors to spread their money into a variety of risk and returns.